Light All Around Us

Sources of Light

Daniel Nunn

Heinemann
LIBRARY
Chicago, Illinois

www.capstonepub.com
Visit our website to find out more information about Heinemann-Raintree books.

To order:

☎ Phone 800-747-4992

🖳 Visit www.capstonepub.com to browse our catalog and order online.

Edited by Dan Nunn, Rebecca Rissman, and Siân Smith
Designed by Marcus Bell
Picture research by Tracy Cummins
Production by Victoria Fitzgerald
Originated by Capstone Global Library Ltd
Printed in the United States of America in Eau Claire, Wisconsin.
051117 010518RP

Library of Congress Cataloging-in-Publication Data
Nunn, Daniel.
  Sources of light / Daniel Nunn.
      p. cm.—(Light all around us)
  Includes bibliographical references and index.
  ISBN 978-1-4329-6621-8 (hb)—ISBN 978-1-4329-6626-3 (pb) 1. Light sources—Juvenile literature. I. Title.
  QC360.N87 2012
   535—dc23   2011041316

Acknowledgments
We would like to thank the following for permission to reproduce images: Getty Images pp.4 (Comstock), 5 (Bruce Laurance), 12 (Fabrice Lerouge), 14 (Holger Leue), 17, 23d (Science Faction/William Radcliffe); istockphoto p.13 (© digitalskillet); Shutterstock pp.6 (© photobank.ch), 7 (© Amma Cat), 8a (© Elenamiv), 8b (© a123luha), 8c (© Rido), 9a (© R-O-M-A), 9c (© Valentina R.), 9d (© Coprid), 10 (© Hydromet), 11 (© Kapu1), 15 (© John Wollwerth), 16 (© Zinaida), 18 (© Rovenko Design), 19 (© mark cinotti), 20 (© fairy_tale), 21 (© greenland), 21 (© dedi), 22a (© Triff), 22b (© windu), 22c (© Susan Montgomery), 22d (© Vadim Ponomarenko), 22e (© Mike Flippo), 22f (© Luminis), 23a (© mark cinotti), 23b (© Zinaida), 23c (© Kapu1).

Cover photograph of a girl with a lantern by a lake reproduced with permission of Corbis (© Don Mason). Back cover photograph of different light sources in a room reproduced with permission of Shutterstock (Amma Cat).

We would like to thank David Harrison, Nancy Harris, Dee Reid, and Diana Bentley for their assistance in the preparation of this book.

Every effort has been made to contact copyright holders of material reproduced in this book. Any omissions will be rectified in subsequent printings if notice is given to the publishers.

Contents

What Is Light?

Light lets us see things.

Light bounces off things and passes into our eyes. This is how we can see things.

Sources of Light

light

light

Light comes from different places.

We call these sources of light.

Sources of light make their own light.

If an object does not make light, it is not a source of light.

Sunlight

Sun

The Sun makes its own light.

Sunlight is very bright.

Never look straight at the Sun.

It is so bright it can hurt your eyes.

Starlight and Moonlight

A star makes its own light.

Stars twinkle in the night sky.

The Moon does not make its
own light.

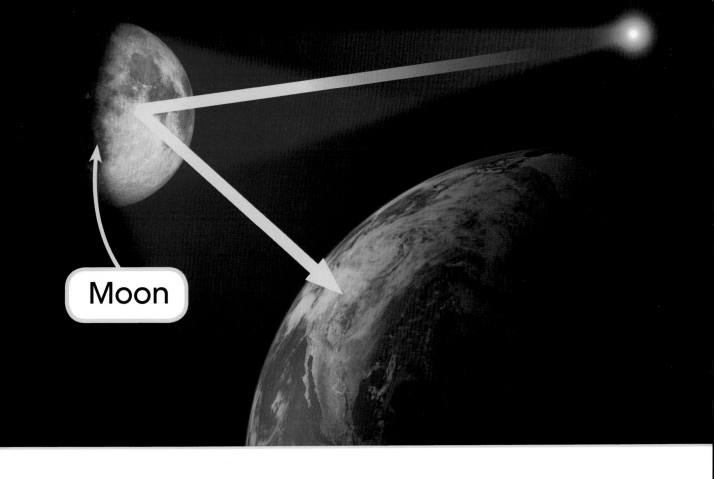

Moon

The Moon reflects or bounces light from the Sun.

Light Made by People

Some sources of light are made by people.

A lightbulb makes light using electricity.

flame

A candle makes light using
a flame.

Traffic lights and televisions are
sources of light, too.

Spot the Sources of Light

Three of these things are sources of light. Can you spot them?

Answer on page 24

Picture Glossary

electricity a form of energy used to make lightbulbs work

Moon a large object in space that goes around Earth

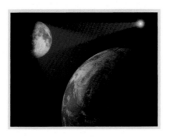

reflect when light bounces off the surface of an object

Sun the star closest to Earth

Index

Answer to question on page 22
The three sources of light are: the Sun, the traffic light, and the flashlight.

Notes for Parents and Teachers

Before reading
Explain to the children that light comes from sources of light. Ask them to look around the room and identify as many sources of light as possible. Are there any that they missed? Or did they name any that are NOT sources of light? Can they distinguish sources of light made by people and natural sources of light? Which do they think is the most important (i.e., the Sun)?

After reading
- Shine a flashlight onto a mirror. Ask the children if they can identify any sources of light. If anyone suggests the mirror, explain that the mirror is not itself a source of light, but rather it is reflecting light from the flashlight.
- Ask the children if they can think of any objects in the sky that are sources of light (the Sun, the stars). The Moon is NOT a source of light. In fact it is acting like the mirror in the first example—it is reflecting the light of the Sun.